DATE DUE

PRINTED IN U.S.A.

Fast Food & the Obesity Epidemic

Understanding Obesity

Fast Food & the Obesity Epidemic

Autumn Libal

Mason Crest

Mason Crest
450 Parkway Drive, Suite D
Broomall, PA 19008
www.masoncrest.com

Printed in the United States of America.

Series ISBN: 978-1-4222-3056-5
ISBN: 978-1-4222-3061-9
ebook ISBN: 978-1-4222-8844-3

Cataloging-in-Publication Data on file with the Library of Congress.

Contents

KEY ICONS TO LOOK FOR:

Text-Dependent Questions: These questions send the reader back to the text for more careful attention to the evidence presented there.

Words to Understand: These words with their easy-to-understand definitions will increase the reader's understanding of the text, while building vocabulary skills.

Series Glossary of Key Terms: This back-of-the book glossary contains terminology used throughout this series. Words found here increase the reader's ability to read and comprehend higher-level books and articles in this field.

Research Projects: Readers are pointed toward areas of further inquiry connected to each chapter. Suggestions are provided for projects that encourage deeper research and analysis.

Sidebars: This boxed material within the main text allows readers to build knowledge, gain insights, explore possibilities, and broaden their perspectives by weaving together additional information to provide realistic and holistic perspectives.

Introduction

We as a society often reserve our harshest criticism for those conditions we understand the least. Such is the case with obesity. Obesity is a chronic and often-fatal disease that accounts for 300,000 deaths each year. It is second only to smoking as a cause of premature death in the United States. People suffering from obesity need understanding, support, and medical assistance. Yet what they often receive is scorn.

Today, children are the fastest growing segment of the obese population in the United States. This constitutes a public health crisis of enormous proportions. Living with childhood obesity affects self-esteem, employment, and attainment of higher education. But childhood obesity is much more than a social stigma. It has serious health consequences.

Childhood obesity increases the risk for poor health in adulthood and premature death. Depression, diabetes, asthma, gallstones, orthopedic diseases, and other obesity-related conditions are all on the rise in children. Over the last 20 years, more children are being diagnosed with type 2 diabetes—a leading cause of preventable blindness, kidney failure, heart disease, stroke, and amputations. Obesity is undoubtedly the most pressing nutritional disorder among young people today.

This series is an excellent first step toward understanding the obesity crisis and profiling approaches for remedying it. If we are to reverse obesity's current trend, there must be family, community, and national objectives promoting healthy eating and exercise. As a nation, we must demand broad-based public-health initiatives to limit TV watching, curtail junk food advertising toward children, and promote physical activity. More than rhetoric, these need to be our rallying cry. Anything short of this will eventually fail, and within our lifetime obesity will become the leading cause of death in the United States if not in the world.

Victor F. Garcia, M.D.
Founder, Bariatric Surgery Center
Cincinnati Children's Hospital Medical Center
Professor of Pediatrics and Surgery
School of Medicine
University of Cincinnati

Words to Understand

corporations: Businesses made up of groups of people authorized to act as a single body.

assembly line: An arrangement of machines and workers in which a task moves from operation to operation until it is complete.

conglomerate: A mass formed of diverse things or parts.

mass-produced: Made in large quantities at a time.

entrepreneurs: People who start their own businesses.

franchises: Individuals or groups who have been given permission by a company to sell its goods or services.

uniformity: The state of being the same, consistent, or unchanging.

dehydrating: Preserving food by removing the moisture from it; drying.

sociologist: Someone who studies the development, structure, interaction, and collective behavior of organized groups of human beings.

inherently: At the core; essentially; naturally.

perpetuated: Aided or helped to continue.

Chapter 1

The Birth of a Nation?

America's Obesity Crisis

Look around. The signs are everywhere: they're in the headlines of newspapers, the titles of bestselling books, the lead stories on the nightly news, and the bodies of people all around you. In America today, obesity—the state of being very overweight—is not simply a problem, it's a national crisis.

Think that's an exaggeration? It's not. Two out of every three American adults are overweight, with one out of three officially obese. And adults aren't the only ones suffering. One out of every six people between the ages of six and nineteen is also overweight, with an additional one out of six in danger of becoming overweight. The numbers (along with our waistlines) are still growing. Experts now fear that obesity will soon be even more than a crisis; it will be the American way of life.

So how did Americans get to be the heaviest people on earth? Are individuals to blame for ballooning buttocks and walloping waistlines? Are Americans more irresponsible than people of all other societies? Do we care less about our health than anyone else? If American obesity rates increase every year, does that mean that each year we become less and less concerned with the way we eat, feel, and look?

On the one hand, as the heads of fast food **corporations** and their marketing groups love to remind us, we do make our own personal decisions every time we put a piece of food into our mouths or decide to watch television instead of take a walk. On the other hand, Americans certainly have not decided that they want to be obese. In fact, each year Americans pour billions of dollars into trying to lose weight. We might be the heaviest people in the world, but we also spend the most money trying to slim down.

So why can't we? Why does the obesity crisis keep looming larger? Why are young people now gaining weight at an astonishing rate when they are constantly bombarded by images telling them to be impossibly beautiful and impossibly thin? Clearly, there are other forces at work: forces that encourage us to make unhealthy lifestyle choices, forces that sometimes make it impossible to do anything else.

Although there are a number of factors behind America's bulging bodies, fast food is one of the biggest. In this book, we will explore fast food's role in the American obesity crisis. Along the way, you will learn how the fast-food industry has shaped not only our bodies but our society. Many experts agree: we Americans do not simply eat fast foods. We lead fast-food lifestyles, and this is killing us.

A Legend Is Born: The Assembly-Line Mentality

Believe it or not, many of the ideas that would create fast food did not originate in the food industry at all. They originated in the car industry. In 1913, Henry Ford, that famous American who brought affordable cars to working-class people, created a moving **assembly line** for his car factory. In so doing, he changed American industry and the world. What made Ford's cars affordable was a revolutionary concept of labor division. Prior to Ford's assembly line, every automobile was handcrafted from start to finish resulting in a unique, one-of-a-kind vehicle. This was an incredibly labor-intensive and time-consuming undertaking that required highly skilled (and expensive) craftspeople.

Henry Ford believed he could make cars in a more efficient and cost-effective way. To do so, he imagined the automobile as a **conglomerate** of different components or parts. These parts were **mass-produced** to be identical and interchangeable. (For example, the engine in one car was identical to the engine in every other car and could therefore be put in any car.) The work of putting an automobile together was likewise broken down into all its different components, and one person was assigned to each task. This eliminated the need for expensive skilled labor because workers no longer needed to know how to build a complete car. They just needed to know how to perform one task, like tightening a specific bolt or putting on a tire. To save time, Ford put the cars on an assembly line. Now workers never even wasted time walking around. The cars just rolled to them, they performed their specific tasks, and off the cars went down the line. The result was amazing: a huge increase in production, a dramatic decrease in production costs, and a steady supply of cars that average Americans could afford. Within twenty years, well over fifteen million automobiles had been sold in the United States, and American society had changed forever.

The McDonald's Story

In 1948, Richard and Maurice McDonald applied Henry Ford's principle for building cars to making food. In his book *Fast Food Nation: The Dark Side of the All-American Meal,* awarding-winning journalist Eric Schlosser explains the rise of McDonald's and the fast-food industry. In what they called their "Speedee Service System," the McDonald brothers removed any food that needed silverware from their menu (this left the basics like hamburgers, fries, and milk shakes), standardized the menu (all the hamburgers would be cooked and served exactly the same way, and customers could not get substitutions), and divided the food preparation into tasks with each task being performed by one person. The McDonald brothers no longer needed skilled cooks; they just needed people who could put burgers on a grill, lower fries into hot oil, or run a milk shake machine. If workers needed fewer skills and less training, then they could also be paid less money. Furthermore, by doing away with plates and silverware and wrapping all the food in paper or other disposable products, the McDonalds eliminated the need for dishwashers and the cost of dishes and equipment, another labor-reducing, money-saving move. With their new system, the McDonalds could make food faster and cheaper than anyone else, allowing them to undercut competitors' prices and still make enough profit to get rich. Fast food was born.

Today we are so accustomed to prepared, prepackaged, fast foods, that the McDonalds' system doesn't seem revolutionary. In fact, you might well think it's the only logical way for a restaurant to run. How else would a restaurant get its food made and delivered to its customers in a fast and affordable manner? Well, that's exactly the point: before the McDonald brothers introduced this system, food preparation was time-consuming and expensive. Although at the time, drive-in restaurants were extremely popular (especially with young people), restaurants simply weren't affordable for

Fast food (n). *Food that is wholly or partially prepared for quick sale or serving, especially in a snack bar or restaurant.*

families to eat at on a regular basis. If you were a single person, you might be able to save your pennies for a night out with friends, but if you were a family with children, dinner at a restaurant would be a rare, special, or perhaps nonexistent event. With cheaper fast food, however, a family could now afford to go out to dinner. It was still much more expensive than making dinner at home, but the occasional night out at McDonald's wasn't going to break the bank.

Soon customers were lining up around the block for a McDonald's hamburger, and restaurant owners and **entrepreneurs** from around the country were traveling to see the McDonald's Speedee Service System with their own eyes. After witnessing the food-production miracle, they began opening fast-food restaurants of their own, each trying to improve on the others' ideas. Fast-food restaurant owners soon knew that the key to fast food was preparation and mechanization. The more the foods could be prepared ahead of time, the quicker they could be served up when ordered; and the more specialized machines they could invent, the less they needed to rely on people to cook the food. Soon machines that cooked two sides of a burger at once, mixed numerous milk shakes at a time, or performed other amazing tasks were simplifying the work, eliminating the need for numerous employees, reducing wages, and reducing the cost of the final product.

Moving Across the Nation: The Evolution of Fast Food

A few years after the McDonald brothers introduced their Speedee Service System, a man named Ray Kroc paid them a visit. Mr. Kroc was the salesman who sold the milk shake machines McDonald's used. He couldn't understand why any restaurant needed six milk shake machines, each capable of making five shakes at a time. When Kroc saw the line outside McDonald's, however, he suddenly understood this was an altogether different operation than any he had ever seen.

Ray Kroc didn't have much education—he had dropped out of high school and never attended college—but he had a real gift for sales. Soon he was giving Richard and Maurice the sales pitch of his life. If they sold him the right to open McDonald's **franchises**, Kroc said, he would make them rich. Richard and Maurice, however, were already rich. Their one little restaurant was bringing money in hand over fist, and they didn't really care to work any harder. Now they preferred to enjoy life and the prosperity it brought. But when it came to making a sale, Ray Kroc was the best. He assured the McDonald brothers there wouldn't be any more work for them. All they had to do was sit back and watch the money roll in.

Although Richard and Maurice McDonald introduced the Speedee Service System, Ray Kroc made McDonald's what it is today. Kroc realized that America was fundamentally different from the country it had been just a few decades ago. It was the age of the automobile. Gone were the days of being born, living, and dying in the same town. Americans were now mobile, and as highways stretched across the country, people were enjoying their new freedom. Ray Kroc dreamed that no matter where Americans traveled, there

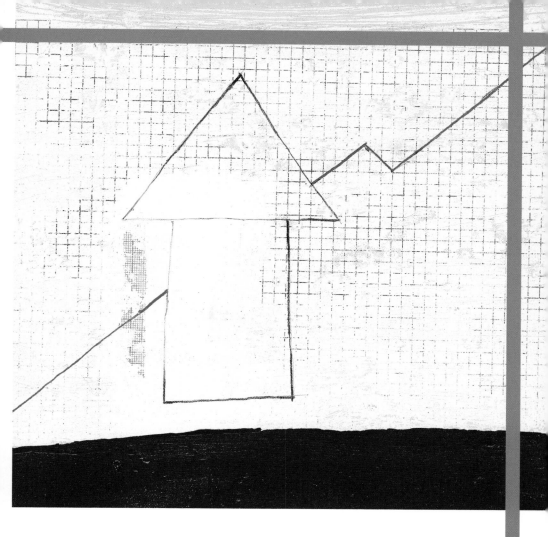

would be a McDonald's on the horizon. Kroc suspected that people arriving in an unfamiliar town would be more likely to go to a McDonald's, where they knew exactly what would be on the menu, than to the local mom-and-pop restaurant they knew nothing about. Kroc believed the key to McDonald's success would be **uniformity**. No matter who opened a McDonald's franchise or where in America it was located, it would guarantee the same menu and service as every other McDonald's in America.

Soon McDonald's restaurants were opening all over the country. Menu items were added, and operating systems were perfected. With the company's huge growth, however, uniformity became both more important and more difficult to achieve. How could Kroc ensure that a hamburger served in a California McDonald's tasted exactly the same as a hamburger served across the country in a New York McDonald's? If the food was going to be identical, it had to all come from the same place and be prepared in exactly the same way. Huge offsite facilities rose, all capable of mass-producing enough McDonald's food to supply hundreds of restaurants nationwide. Now McDonald's food was prepared, prepackaged, and in many cases precooked, before it even entered the restaurant's kitchen. It was then preserved and shipped to all corners of America. This food preservation was key to the McDonald's system's success, and it wouldn't have been possible without the incredible advances in technology being made at the time. New methods of freezing, packaging, **dehydrating**, and other forms of food preservation ensured food didn't spoil before arriving at a McDonald's kitchen.

For years, other fast-food chains copied whatever McDonald's did, and its practices became the standards by which the entire fast-food industry was run. But businesses outside the fast-food industry also saw the potential profitability of the McDonald's business style. Within a decade, all kinds of companies, from clothing retailers to hotels to construction companies, were adopting McDonald's business principles, creating huge quantities of product offsite, mechanizing and simplifying operations to reduce labor costs, opening franchises all over the country, and guaranteeing that goods and services would be identical no matter where they were purchased. For the rest of the twentieth century, the fast-food industry's operating methods shaped American business; the opening of franchises and big-box stores all over the country shaped the American landscape; and the affordability of their products and services ran America's small businesses into bankruptcy. In 1983, **sociologist** George Ritzer dubbed these changes the "McDonaldization of Society."

Today it seems like there's a fast-food restaurant on every corner of every town. McDonald's, Burger King, Kentucky Fried Chicken, Wendy's, Taco Bell, Pizza Hut, Subway, Arby's, Hardee's, Roy Rogers, Dairy Queen, Dunkin' Donuts, Krispy Kreme, A&W, Domino's, Long John Silver's, and countless more compete for Americans' business. Then there are the semi-fast-food restaurants: Olive Garden, Red Lobster, Friendly's, Denny's, Ruby Tuesdays, Applebee's, Pizzeria Uno, Cracker Barrel, Chili's, LongHorn Steakhouse, Hard Rock Café—all restaurants that combine fast-food principles (like precooked, prepackaged foods) with a sit-down restaurant atmosphere.

What's more, fast food isn't just in restaurants; it's in grocery stores as well. Gone are the days of making everything from scratch. Remember those amazing advances in food storage technology we mentioned a moment ago? Well, they didn't just change the restaurant business. They fundamentally changed our relationship with food. Today you can buy just about any food—from french fries to salad to chicken cordon bleu—already prepared, prepackaged, precooked, and bagged, boxed, canned, dehydrated, or frozen. Fast food has become a way of life.

So is fast food **inherently** bad? It certainly doesn't have to be, and the innovations in appliances, food preparation, food preservation, and other

The J. R. Simplot Company provides the majority of McDonald's french fries. Each day, its plant in Idaho turns approximately one million pounds of potatoes into french fries.

Make Connections:
How Is Obesity Determined?

One tool doctors use to evaluate body size is body mass index (BMI). BMI is a mathematical formula that uses weight and height to determine whether someone's body is a healthy size. The formula for people over twenty is as follows:

[Weight in pounds ÷ (Height in inches x Height in inches)] x 703 = BMI

A BMI that is:
Below 18.5 = Underweight
18.5 – 24.9 = Normal
25.0 – 29.9 = Overweight
30.0 and above = Obese

Example for a person who weighs 132 pounds and is five feet four inches (64 inches) tall:
[132 pounds ÷ (64 inches x 64 inches)] x 703 = 22.66 (a normal weight)

If you are twenty or under, you will need to use the charts on the CDC website: www.cdc.gov/healthyweight/assessing/bmi/childrens_bmi/about_childrens_bmi.html

Research Project

Use the Internet to look into the history of McDonald's. Find out if people liked eating at McDonald's right away, and where the first McDonald's was built by Richard and Maurice McDonald. When did Ray Kroc offer to make a chain out of the restaurant? Find out why people still choose to eat at McDonald's, even though many of them know how unhealthy the food is.

time-, labor-, and cost-saving techniques that appeared with the fast-food age have been blessings to frazzled working parents everywhere. But there is a big problem. Processed foods, especially those served in fast-food restaurants, are often unhealthy. Not only are they often low in nutrients, they are also usually high in fat, salt, and sugar. Despite a current trend by fast-food restaurants to improve their images by offering "healthy" menu alternatives, in general, fast food is still about the worst thing you could possibly eat.

Yet Americans eat lots of it. On an average day, fast-food restaurants serve approximately one out of four American adults. Children and teenagers are also big fast-food consumers. Most eat food from a fast-food restaurant at least once a week, and plenty of American families eat at fast-food restaurants more than once each week. Add vending machines, snack foods, and all the processed foods that are purchased in grocery stores and served at home, and most of us eat at least one form of fast food every day.

Fast-food manufacturers claim they have nothing to do with America's current obesity crisis and that individuals must take personal responsibility

Make Connections:
How Else Is Obesity Determined?

BMI is not always an accurate measure of health. Muscle tissue is much denser and heavier than fat tissue. Since BMI only measures height and weight, an extremely muscular and fit person could have the same BMI as an unfit person who has a large amount of fat. For this reason, a better measure of overweight and obesity is body fat percentage—the amount of your body's tissue that is made of fat. Doctors, nutritionists, and fitness experts use tools to measure different areas of the body. These measurements yield one's body fat percentage.

Body Fat Percentages

Essential Fat: Women 10–12%, Men 2–4%
Athletes: Women 14–20%, Men 6–13%
Fitness: Women 21–24%, Men 14–17%
Acceptable: Women 25–31%, Men 18–25%
Obese: Women 32% +,   Men 25% +

Text-Dependent Questions:

1. How is the assembly line, created by Henry Ford, connected with fast food?
2. Why weren't families able to eat out at restaurants often before McDonald's?
3. Why did Ray Kroc believe opening chains of restaurants across America would be such a success?
4. How did McDonald's affect other American businesses, like clothing stores and hotels?
5. Why is it unhealthy to eat fast food on a regular basis?

for their own health. If individuals choose to eat unhealthy foods, manufacturers claim, that's a person's own choice to make.

Choice, however, is not always as simple as it sounds. To make good choices, you need good information. Far too many people in America today simply don't have the right information to make healthy choices about the food they eat. Widespread misinformation about what is and is not healthy (misinformation that is often spread or **perpetuated** by companies, individuals, or even government organizations who stand to profit from the choices you make) is contributing to America's obesity crisis.

To make healthy eating choices, you need to know what your body really needs on a daily basis. Before we examine what's in all that fast food we're eating, let's explore some of the basics of good nutrition.

Words to Understand

metabolizes: Processes; breaks down into useful components.

facilitate: Bring about.

molecular: Of or consisting of molecules, which are the smallest fundamental unit of a chemical compound.

inclination: Tendency toward something.

Chapter 2

Energy Is the Key: An Introduction to Calories

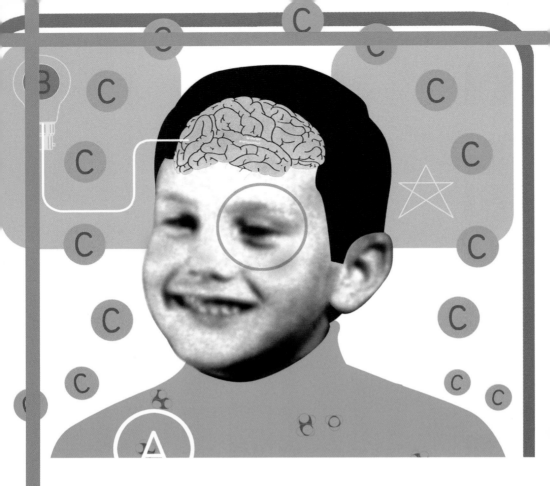

Your Body's Power Plant

Every moment of every day, your body is using energy. You could think of your body as a power plant. A power plant takes in a raw material and processes that material in a way that releases energy. For example, some power plants take in coal, which is burned to heat water. The heated water turns to steam, and the steam puts pressure on turbines, causing them to spin, thus producing electricity. This electricity then powers the lights in the power plant, other machinery, the computers in people's offices, the refrigerator that holds the workers' lunches, and all kinds of other things necessary to keep the power plant running properly and in good condition. Similarly, your body takes in raw materials in the form of food and **metabolizes** those materials to build your body's bones, muscles, and other tissues, create energy, and supply the chemicals that **facilitate** your body's functions. Carbohydrates, fats, and proteins provide your body's power plant with the energy it needs; vitamins, minerals, and water supply other essential ingredients for growth and life.

The Calorie: The Fuel You Burn

Food comes in many **molecular** forms, and some forms of food have more stored energy than others. We measure the amount of energy in food with a unit called a Calorie. Some people think they need 2,000 Calories each day to keep their body powerhouses fueled. This is a misconception. If you look at the average nutrition label on a box of food, you will probably see the phrase "Based on a 2,000 Calorie diet." A 2,000 Calorie diet, however, is just a convenient average that people use to measure the approximate nutrient proportions in food. In reality, however, different people need different amounts of Calories. In fact, the amount of Calories you need each day could be anywhere from 1,500 to 3,900 Calories depending on your age, sex, size, body type, and activity level. For example, teenagers, males, people with large bodies, and very active people usually require more Calories than older people, females, people with small bodies, or people who are inactive. According to the United States Department of Agriculture (USDA), a general estimate for teenage girls and active women is approximately 2,200 Calories each day, while a general estimate for teenage boys and active men is approximately 2,800 Calories each day. These, however, are only averages. It doesn't mean that you must eat and burn exactly the same number of Calories every day. One day you might eat more Calories than you burn, and the extra Calories will be stored as fat. This is not necessarily bad, because a couple days later you might burn more Calories than you eat. Your body will dip into those fat reserves to get the extra energy you need.

How Many Calories Do You Need?

Most people do not count exactly how many Calories they take in every day and measure how many Calories they are burning. This involves some very complicated mathematics and can require the help of health professionals. Luckily, the human body is an amazing thing, and it has many ways of letting you know about its needs. If you need more Calories, you will feel hungry. If you have had enough, you will feel full. But these mechanisms aren't foolproof. Your body can easily get confused. For example, if a person routinely eats when he is not hungry or past the point of being full, he may lose his ability to recognize his natural hunger and fullness signals. His body will also get used to having this large amount of food and may start sending hunger messages when that food is withheld, even if those extra Calories aren't needed. Similarly, if someone routinely ignores her hunger, her body may stop sending hunger signals even though it needs more Calories.

Hunger, however, isn't just about how much you eat. It's also about what you eat. You might be eating many Calories a day, but if most of those Calories are empty of essential nutrients, your body may keep telling you it's hungry.

Hunger is only one of the signals your body can give you. Weight is another. If you are taking in more Calories than you are burning, you will gain weight. If you are taking in fewer Calories than you are burning, you will

Make Connections: The Measurement of Food Energy

A Calorie is a thermal unit of energy; it is an amount of heat. Calorie with a capital "C" stands for large calorie or kilogram calorie. This is the type of Calorie used to measure energy in food. One Calorie is equal to the amount of energy it would take to heat one kilogram of water (approximately one liter or four and a quarter cups) one degree Celsius. There is also a measurement known as a small calorie, or calorie with a lowercase "c." This type of calorie is used in chemistry, physics, and other disciplines that need to accurately measure tiny amounts of heat. A small calorie is the amount of heat it takes to heat one gram of water (one milliliter or about 20 drops from an eyedropper) one degree Celsius. There are one thousand small calories in a single food Calorie. That's a lot of energy!

lose weight. It is important to remember, however, that weight gain or loss only tells you if you are burning what you take in; it does not tell you how many Calories you need. For example, perhaps you are using the same number of Calories you take in every day and are therefore neither gaining nor losing weight. You could still, however, be getting too few Calories. If so, you

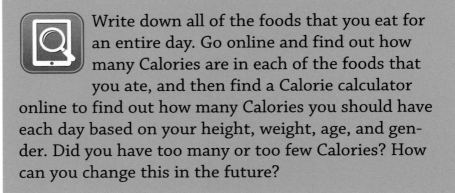

Research Project

Write down all of the foods that you eat for an entire day. Go online and find out how many Calories are in each of the foods that you ate, and then find a Calorie calculator online to find out how many Calories you should have each day based on your height, weight, age, and gender. Did you have too many or too few Calories? How can you change this in the future?

would feel tired, run down, and unable to perform numerous physical activities. If you ate more Calories, you would find you had more energy, could be more active, and still burn all the Calories you take in. Similarly, perhaps you are taking in more Calories each day than you burn and are therefore gaining

Each gram of carbohydrate you consume will give your body four Calories. Each gram of protein also gives your body four Calories. Each gram of fat, the most concentrated form of food energy, gives your body nine Calories.

Text-Dependent Questions:

1. How are energy and Calories connected?
2. What are two reasons that your body may tell you it is still hungry, even if it has gotten enough Calories?
3. What happens if you take in more Calories than you are burning?
4. What if you take in fewer Calories than you are burning?
5. Why might exercising sometimes be a better way to lose weight than cutting back on Calories?

excess weight. Your first **inclination** might be to cut back on your caloric intake, but perhaps the real problem is that you are not getting enough exercise. In this case, increasing your activity without cutting back on Calories could be the answer to achieving good health. When a person is having trouble finding the right balance between caloric intake and energy expenditure, seeking advice from a health professional such as a doctor, nurse, nutritionist, or fitness instructor is often a good idea.

Knowing approximately how many Calories you should take in each day is only part of the story. You also need to know where those Calories should come from. Calories come in three basic forms: carbohydrates (or sugars), proteins, and fats. The next chapter will take a deeper look at healthy eating.

Words to Understand

hormone: A chemical that regulates activity and processes within the body.

heart disease: A disease characterized by the clogging of arteries in the heart.

colon cancer: Cancer of the lower part of the intestine.

insoluble: Does not dissolve.

soluble: Capable of being dissolved.

toxins: Poisons.

plaque: Fatty deposits that build up in the arteries.

legumes: A family of plants including peas, beans, and lentils, with nitrogen-bearing modules on their roots.

exploit: Take advantage of for one's own ends.

Chapter 3

Variety Is the Spice of Life: Getting Your Essential Nutrients

- Carbohydrates
- Fats
- Protein
- Vitamins and Minerals

It's easy to get confused when reading about nutrition. Everyone seems to have an opinion, and these opinions are often contradictory. One person says carbohydrates are good for you while another person says they are bad for you. One person says fat is good for you while another says it is bad for you. One diet plan says you should eat lots of meat. Another says you should eat no animal products at all. Good nutrition, however, is far too complicated to sum up in a one-liner. The truth is that every day your body needs energy and nutrients from a variety of sources, and few foods can be labeled all bad or all good.

Carbohydrates

Carbohydrates are sugars, and they are found in numerous foods such as grain products, fruits, vegetables, other plant products, and even candy. According to the National Academy of Sciences, between 45 and 65 percent of your daily Calories should come from carbohydrates. Not all carbohydrates, however, are the same, and some are much better for you than others. The healthiest carbohydrates are *complex carbohydrates*. They are composed of sugar chains that may be hundreds of molecules long. Usually, complex carbohydrates don't taste like sugar at all.

Complex carbohydrates are found in whole-grain foods like whole-wheat bread and long-grain brown rice. Your body, however, can't use these carbohydrates in this complex form. Instead, it must convert the complex sugars into a simple sugar called glucose. Glucose is the fuel for your body and mind. Every part of your body, from the muscles in your toes to the brain in your head, uses glucose for energy. To obtain glucose, your body breaks the complex carbohydrate chains down molecule by molecule. This takes a very long time, supplying your body with a sustained source of energy. As each glucose molecule becomes available, it gets picked up by a **hormone** called insulin.

The insulin carries the glucose molecule into a cell where it gets "burned" for energy.

In addition to being a good source of energy, complex carbohydrates are an excellent source of essential nutrients like vitamins, minerals, and fiber. Fiber is a carbohydrate, but its molecular structure is so complex your body cannot break it down. Just because fiber cannot be broken down into energy doesn't mean that it's not good for you. In fact, fiber is absolutely essential to your good health and may even prevent conditions like **heart disease** and **colon cancer**.

But how can something your body cannot digest be good for you? Because fiber performs an important job in your digestive tract. The two types of fiber—**insoluble** and **soluble**—each have their own benefits. Insoluble fiber acts like a plow, pushing through your intestines and shoving everything it encounters along the way out of your body. Soluble fiber acts more like a sponge, sucking up things (like fat, cholesterol, and naturally or artificially

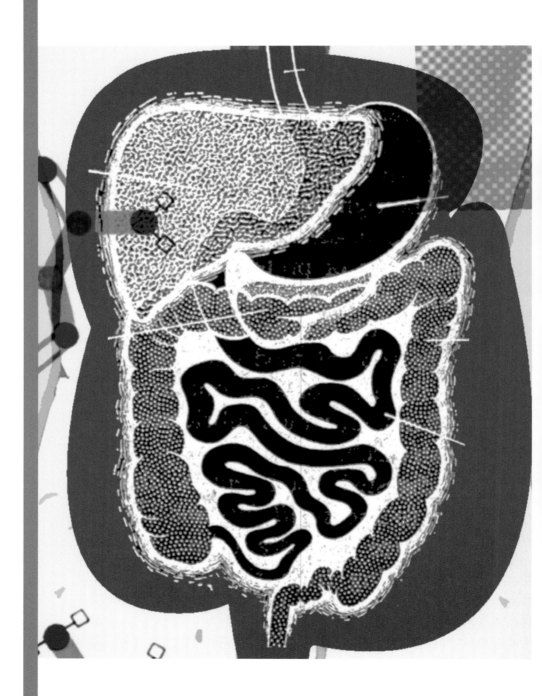

occurring toxins in your food) and carrying them out. If you are not getting enough fiber, digested foods and waste products can sit in your intestines for days . . . or even longer. The results, as you can probably imagine, may not be pretty. Lack of fiber can cause constipation—when waste backs up in the intestines. Any **toxins** present in your food waste will stay in contact with your intestine's cells and may even be absorbed into the body. Some scientists believe that this prolonged exposure to toxins in your body's wastes may be a leading cause of colon cancer. Fiber's ability to absorb toxins and excess fats and flush waste from your body ultimately reduces your risk for this cancer and other illnesses.

Unlike complex carbohydrates and fiber, which should be plentiful in your diet, some carbohydrates should be avoided. These are simple carbohydrates. Simple carbohydrates are only two or three sugar molecules long. Instead of being converted to glucose slowly, simple carbohydrates are broken down all

Foods that are high in fiber include whole oats, long-grain brown rice, beans, broccoli, apples, figs, prunes, green leafy vegetables, and fruit and vegetable skins. The American Gastroenterological Association recommends that adults get an average of 30 to 35 grams of fiber each day. Currently American adults get an average of only 11 grams per day.

at once, flooding your body with glucose and causing your blood-sugar levels to spike.

Think for a moment about a spring snowmelt. As the weather warms, the ice and snow on the ground will change to water. Water is, generally speaking, good for the earth. If the weather warms slowly, the snow will melt slowly, and the ground will be able to absorb all the water. If, however, the weather warms up all at once, the snow will melt too quickly. The earth won't be able to absorb the sudden rush of water, and the water will flow over the ground, flood the rivers, wash away topsoil, and perhaps cause major destruction. The difference between the way complex carbohydrates and simple carbohydrates break down in your body is a like the difference between a gradual snowmelt and a sudden snowmelt. A slow release of sugar is essential for sustained energy. A flood of sugar is bad for your body and

Make Connections: Carbohydrates

To figure out how many grams of carbohydrates you should eat each day, multiply the number of Calories you need by .50. Divide the result by four (the number of Calories in a gram of carbohydrate). This gives you the low-end of your necessary carbohydrate intake. Now multiply the number of Calories by .60, and divide the answer by four. This gives you the high-end of your necessary carbohydrate intake. Here is an example for a person who requires 2,200 Calories each day:

(2200 Calories x .50) / 4 Calories per gram of carbohydrates = 275 grams
(2200 Calories x .60) / 4 Calories per gram of carbohydrates = 330 grams

A person who requires 2,200 Calories should eat approximately 275 to 330 grams of carbohydrates (mostly complex) every day. These can come from grains like bread, pasta, and rice, but you should also get some of your carbohydrates from fruits and vegetables.

can overwhelm your system. When you eat lots of sugar, your body goes into insulin-production overdrive. The insulin pulls the sugar into your cells, which may cause you to experience a "sugar rush," or sudden surge of energy. Usually, however, your body can't burn this flood of sugar fast enough, so it stores the excess sugar as fat—your body's energy storehouse.

The sugar you find in your sugar bowl, the sugars in processed grain products like white bread, white rice, and white pasta, and the sugars in many fruits are simple sugars. Most fruits are full of good things like vitamins, minerals, and fiber, and their naturally occurring sugars are not nearly as concentrated as the sugars in things like white bread or candy. Fruits, therefore, should be eaten two or three times a day. Processed grain products like white bread and white pasta, however, have extremely large concentrations of simple sugars and have had almost all their fiber and other nutrients removed; they are high-Calorie foods, but their Calories are "empty." Unlike fruits, these highly refined carbohydrates as well as highly refined sugar should be used very sparingly and should not be eaten every day.

 ## Fats

According to the National Academy of Sciences, about 20 to 35 percent of your Calories should come from fats. Fats are the most concentrated form of food energy, yielding nine Calories per gram, so it takes far fewer grams of fat than carbohydrates to give you a high dose of Calories. Some fats are very good for you and necessary for maintaining health and body functions. Other types of fat can be extremely dangerous, especially when consumed in large amounts.

Fat falls into two basic categories: saturated and unsaturated. Saturated fats are solid at room temperature, while unsaturated fats are liquid at room temperature. Saturated fats come mostly from animals and should be eaten in moderation because they contain cholesterol.

Cholesterol is an essential part of cell membranes and nervous system

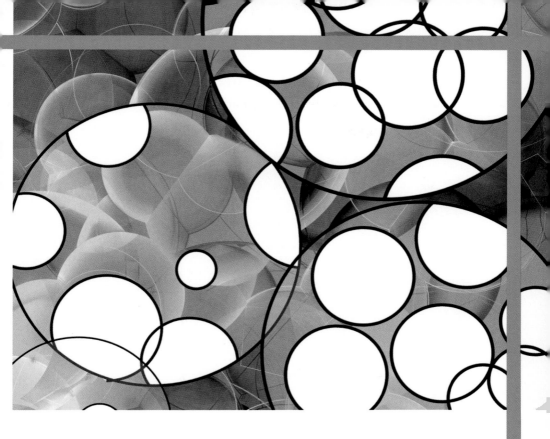

tissues, but this doesn't mean you have to eat foods that contain choles-terol. Your body manufactures its own cholesterol, so eating too much of it can be dangerous. There are two types of cholesterol: *high-density lipopro-teins* (HDL) and *low-density lipoproteins* (LDL). When there is too much LDL cholesterol in your bloodstream, it can build up as **plaque** on your artery walls. Eventually, this plaque can block blood flow, causing cardiovascular disease, heart attack, stroke, and even death. HDL cholesterol, however, is considered good. The HDL molecule has binding sites—places where the LDL cholesterol latches on. The whole group of HDL and LDL molecules can then be easily flushed from the body. You should consume less than 300 milligrams of cholesterol each day, and the less the better. You can decrease your cholesterol intake by decreasing your saturated fat intake, which should not exceed 20 to 25 grams each day.

You can increase your levels of good cholesterol (HDL) by eating certain

Make Connections: Fat

To find out how many grams of fat you require each day, multiply the number of Calories you need by .20. Divide the resulting number by nine (the number of Calories in each gram of fat). The answer gives you the low-end of your necessary fat intake. Then multiply your daily Calories by .35, and divide the resulting number by nine. This gives you the high-end of your acceptable fat intake. Here is the formula for a person who requires 2,500 Calories each day:

(2500 Calories x .20) ÷ 9 Calories per gram of fat = 55.5 grams of fat
(2500 Calories x .35) ÷ 9 Calories per gram of fat = 97.2 grams of fat

A person who needs 2,500 Calories each day should consume approximately 56 to 97 grams of fat. This should include as little saturated fat as possible.

unsaturated fats. Unsaturated fats come in two forms: monounsaturated and polyunsaturated. Foods like avocados and olive oil are high in monounsaturated fats, while foods like some grains, nuts, and fish are high in polyunsaturated fats. Mono- and polyunsaturated fats are actually good for you. Polyunsaturated fats, especially those found in certain fish (like salmon,

lake trout, tuna, and mackerel), contain a high percentage of HDL cholesterol and can actually lower your blood pressure and reduce your chance of getting heart disease by binding with LDL cholesterol so that it can't form plaque on your arteries. However, despite the fact that unsaturated fats are good for you, they must still be consumed in moderate amounts because they contain a large amount of calories. If eaten in excess, these fat Calories quickly contribute to weight gain.

Protein

According to the National Academy of Sciences, between 10 and 35 percent of your daily Calories should come from protein. Protein, however, isn't just important for the caloric energy it gives you. It is also a major building block for your body. Without protein, your body would not be able to build or repair your muscles and other bodily tissues.

When most people think of protein, they think of meat. Muscle tissue is made of protein, so meat is the densest form of protein you can get, but most plants (especially grains, nuts, and **legumes**) also contain protein. Meat is an expensive food, and in many countries around the world, people cannot afford to eat meat on a regular basis. In the United States, however, many people have enough money to eat meat at least once and even multiple times a day. Americans therefore tend to eat very high-protein diets—but your body can only process a certain amount of protein at any given time. If it is needed, some of the protein will be used to build and repair body tissues. Some of the protein will also be converted to glucose and used as energy or stored as fat. The excess protein will be flushed out of your body.

Today, you may be hearing a lot about high-protein/low-carbohydrate diets. Be careful with what you hear. Many people think high-protein/low-carbohydrate means lots of meat and little bread and plant products. This can be dangerous. As we saw earlier, some carbohydrates can be bad for you and should be eaten sparingly, but cutting out all carbohydrates also cuts out fiber, nutrients, and energy. As mentioned, meat is the densest form of protein, but it can also be very high in saturated fats. Furthermore, as we already stated, meat is not the only source of protein. Legumes are high in protein, but they are also high in fiber. Whole grains are high in protein, but they are also high in complex carbohydrates. A high-protein, low-carbohydrate diet could become extremely unhealthy very quickly if it relied on large amounts

of meat and animal products containing saturated fats and no plant products. On the other hand, a diet that is high in protein from healthy sources like beans, lentils, nuts, whole grains, and fish, and low in simple carbohydrates like white bread, white rice, sugary carbonated beverages, and candy could be extremely healthy.

Vitamins and Minerals

The formula for good health is not as simple as just getting the correct percentages of carbohydrates, fats, and proteins. You also need a whole host of vitamins and minerals. For example, vitamins A and C are important for your immune system. The B vitamins are important for your vision, cardiovascular health, energy, and mood. Vitamin D helps the body metabolize phosphorous and calcium, two minerals that are necessary for strong bones. Without the mineral iron, your blood can't carry oxygen to your cells. Vitamin and mineral deficiencies can cause fatigue, weakness, bone loss, illness, and numerous other problems.

Make Connections: Protein

To find out how much protein you need each day, multiply the number of Calories you need by .10. Divide the answer by four (the number of Calories in one gram of protein). This gives you the low-end of your necessary protein intake. Now multiply your Calories by .35 and divide by four. This answer gives you the high-end of your necessary protein intake. Here is an example for a person who needs 2,500 Calories each day:

(2500 Calories x .10) ÷ 4 Calories per gram of protein = 62.5 grams
(2500 Calories x .35) ÷ 4 Calories per gram of protein = 218.75 grams

A person who needs 2,500 Calories each day should eat approximately 63 to 219 grams of protein.

Vegetables (especially dark leafy greens like kale, spinach, and chard) and fruits, in addition to being a good source of fiber and healthy carbohydrates, are some of your best sources of vitamins and minerals. Fruit is high in sugar, so it is good to limit yourself after eating it two or three times a day. When it comes to most green vegetables, however, you can't get too many. (Some vegetables—like carrots, potatoes, beets, and peas—are also high in sugar.)

And yet most American diets contain few vegetables. Instead, when we're hungry, we tend to go for foods that we like or that are convenient but that don't actually have the nutrients we need. As we will soon see, not only are these processed, convenience, and fast foods devoid of many necessary nutrients, many of them are also packed with things your body doesn't need: salt, sugar, unhealthy fats, and empty calories.

If you're like many people, you might have a sweet tooth, love salty foods, and crave fatty and Calorie-rich foods. In fact, for many of us, fat, salt, and sugar—the things we should eat the least—are also the things we crave the most. We humans can't seem to resist the stuff! But why would your body desire foods that you don't need and that can even be unhealthy for you?

As Michael D. Lemonick, senior science writer at *Time* magazine, reported in a 2004 article, human beings evolved to crave high-Calorie foods like those containing fats and sugars. Life was hard for early humans. We had to catch or find all our food, which was extremely time- and energy-consuming.

Make Connections: Food Guides and Serving Sizes

Most Americans learned about nutrition from the United States Department of Agriculture's (USDA) Food Guide Pyramid, which in 2011 was replaced with MyPlate. Even this new guide has significant problems. For example, it recommends carbohydrates as a basis of a healthy diet, but draws no distinction between complex and simple carbohydrates. It doesn't include fats at all in its recommended diet but some fats (like those in fish and olive oil) are actually good for you.

In response to these shortcomings and inaccuracies, a team of Harvard University researchers designed their own Healthy Eating Plate. It looks quite different. At its base is exercise instead of a food. It recommends the majority of a person's diet consist of complex carbohydrates, healthy fats, and vegetables. It recommends red meats, butter, and simple carbohydrates be used sparingly. It also does away with serving sizes, instead recommending how many times a day people should eat each food. For example, it states whole grains should be eaten "at most meals," and vegetables should be eaten "in abundance." You can learn more about the differences between the USDA's Food Guide Plate and Harvard University's Healthy Eating Plate on the web at www.hsph.harvard.edu/nutritionsource/pyramid.

It was very difficult to have a balanced diet with all the nutrients humans needed. And more food wasn't guaranteed to show up tomorrow. If you had it, you'd better eat as much of it as you could get! Those who ate the most Calories survived, and those who ate the least, well . . . they died. It's only within the last century (and in the wealthiest countries) that food has suddenly become so plentiful and easy for most people to obtain. Our evolution, however, occurred over millions of years in which our bodies told us to eat every Calorie-rich food in sight. It's not easy to give up millions of years of craving—so most people still find the fattiest, saltiest, and most sugary foods to also be the tastiest and most desirable.

Fast food caters to these ancient cravings of ours. But now that we've learned what your body needs on a daily basis, let's look at what's *really* in those fast foods. In the next chapter, we'll see how they **exploit** your body's natural desire for fat, sugar, and salt. We will learn about the numerous circumstances—like farming techniques that create high-fat meat, processing

Text-Dependent Questions:

1. Why are simple carbohydrates not as healthy for you as complex carbohydrates?
2. Why shouldn't you eat foods with a lot of cholesterol?
3. Besides meat, list three other foods that contain protein.
4. Why did people evolve to crave high-Calorie and fatty foods?

that leaches nutrients and taste from the food, and preservatives and additives that are dangerous for your body—that work together to make fast food just about the unhealthiest food you can eat. We will also look at some specific menu items from fast-food industry leaders to see exactly what's in this stuff that we call fast "food" and examine whether eating at fast-food restaurants can really be part of a healthy diet.

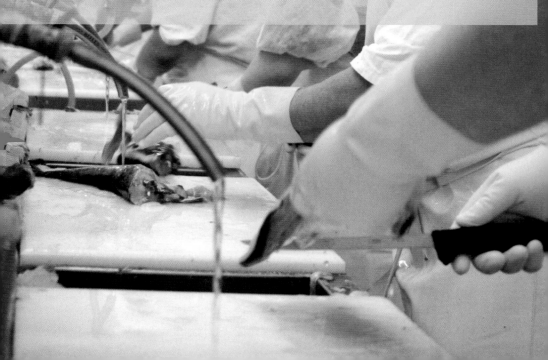

Words to Understand

coagulation: The process by which liquid changes to a semisolid.

amorphous: Shapeless; without form or structure.

reconstituted: Built up again from parts; reconstructed; restored.

leach: Dissolve and pass out of a substance.

enrichment: Improvement in the nutritive quality of food by adding vitamins, minerals, and other nutrients.

trace: Present in tiny, barely detectable amounts.

general practitioner: A doctor who does not specialize in a specific area but treats illnesses of all kinds.

gastroenterologist: A doctor who specializes in disorders and abnormalities of the stomach and intestines.

cardiologist: A doctor who specializes in diseases and abnormalities of the heart.

nutritionist: Someone who specializes in the study of how someone or something uses food substances.

vegan: Containing no animal products.

discloses: Reveals.

phenomenon: An occurrence.

Chapter 4

What You Don't Know Will Hurt You: What's Really in Fast Food

- The Life of Chicken Nuggets: A Lesson in Food Processing

- Toxic Taco, Horrific Hamburger?

- Educating Yourself

The Life of Chicken Nuggets: A Lesson in Food Processing

Have you ever wondered how chicken nuggets are made? The process begins when chicks hatch in an incubator beneath the mechanical warmth of heat lamps. No mother chicken is present, but food and water are available for the chicks. After awhile, hundreds of chicks are placed in a box and huddle together for warmth. The box is opened, and the chicks are now with twenty thousand chicks in a huge room. Lights provide heat, machines provide food and water—and the chicks grow fat.

After six weeks, the food is removed. The chickens are put in giant metal boxes, which are loaded onto trucks and hauled away. After being butchered, thousands of dead chickens are scalded so the heat from boiling water and steam loosen the feathers. Then the feathers are plucked and the entrails, head, and feet are removed.

For many chickens, this would be the last step before packaging and traveling to grocery store shelves. But for the thousands of chickens destined to become nuggets, their meat is cut from the bones, ground up, and mixed together. Chicken skin, salt, water, beef flavoring, and chemicals that cause **coagulation** are added to the pulpy soup. The **amorphous** mixture is squeezed through a tube. Machines shape the little lumps of **reconstituted** protein into nuggets, which travel through flour, seasonings, batter, and bread crumbs before being plunged into deep fryers. Then they are immediately frozen and packaged. The next step is reheating in another deep fryer or an oven, and finally the chicken nuggets are served for dinner.

The elaborate process a chicken undergoes on the way to becoming a chicken nugget is representative of the amount of processing most fast foods go through before they arrive at your table. As with a chicken nugget, many of

these foods hardly resemble in the end what they started out as at the beginning. Throughout food processing, things are both added and lost, and this has serious implications for your health.

To begin with, factory-farmed animals raised on grain-based diets are already higher in fat and often lower in nutrients than wild or free-range animals. Furthermore, many nutrients, like vitamins and minerals, are delicate and volatile. Some degrade when heated. Others degrade when frozen. Some are water soluble and **leach** out of food into its cooking water. Others are fat-soluble and seep out of food into its cooking oil. Some disintegrate over time, while others readily combine with other chemicals, making them unavailable for your body's use. All this spells trouble for the quality of processed foods.

Generally speaking, the closer food is to its original form when you eat it,

the more nutrient-rich it will be. A freshly picked apple will be more nutrient-rich than applesauce out of a can. A bread containing whole grains like barley, cracked wheat, brown rice, and buckwheat will have more nutrients than white flour. A steak will contain more nutrients than a hotdog. By the time fast foods make it through their processing, they have few nutrients and sometimes little taste left to offer. In many foods, especially breads and cereals, vitamins and minerals will be added at the end of the process to make up for some of what has been lost. This **enrichment** process, however, will only replace a few of the nutrients and can't make up for the wide range of benefits (from fiber to **trace** vitamins and minerals) that has been lost.

Along with nutrients, a processed food's taste needs to be restored (or simply created) as well. It's awfully difficult to make something in huge quantities in a factory; freeze, dehydrate, can, box, bottle, or bag it; store it for days, weeks, months, or even years; and have it emerge at the other end tasting good. Fast-food restaurants need the time-saving and cost-reducing qualities of processed foods, but if they want to keep their customers, they can't afford to sacrifice taste. For a customer, the thing that makes fast food desirable is not just that it's fast (though that is nice) but that it tastes oh-so-good. Today, the science of making processed foods taste good is a gigantic industry. In the end, however, four basic things give fast foods their irresistible taste: fat, sugar, salt, and natural and artificial flavors.

Toxic Taco, Horrific Hamburger?

In the 2004 film, *Supersize Me*, Morgan Spurlock conducts a fast-food experiment. He decides to eat nothing but McDonald's food for thirty days. He enlists three doctors—a **general practitioner**, a **gastroenterologist**, and a **cardiologist**—a **nutritionist**, and a fitness expert to track him on his journey. He has blood tests taken and physicals performed. They all report he's in perfect health. Then he sets rules for himself: he must only eat food sold at McDonald's, he must eat three meals every day, he must eat everything on the menu at least once, and if asked if he wants his meal "supersized" he has to say yes.

By the end of the month, Spurlock is in rough shape. He has gained twenty-four pounds, lost muscle strength, fallen into depression, had a huge surge in cholesterol, and his blood tests reveal his liver is close to failure. His doctors are concerned for more than his health; they are concerned for his life. The experiment ends. Spurlock ditches McDonald's, begins an exercise routine, embarks on a **vegan** diet, and works for fourteen months to undo the damage done in just thirty days.

Supersize Me has achieved widespread acclaim—and widespread criticism. The majority of that criticism comes directly from the fast-food industry. McDonald's and other fast-food restaurants cried foul, saying Spurlock's choice to eat nothing but McDonald's food was completely irresponsible and

grossly out of proportion with the average American's consumption of fast food. Fast-food industry leaders claim everyone knows that eating fast food all the time is bad for you and that, since nutrition information for their food is widely available, there is no excuse for individuals to claim they have been misled about the content of these foods. At the same time, industry representatives insist that most fast-food restaurants now offer healthy food options, and there is no reason why fast food can't be part of a healthy diet.

Given the busy lifestyles most Americans now lead, however, one might ask, "Is Spurlock's experiment really all that crazy?" Probably not many people eat at McDonald's three meals a day every day. But plenty of people rely on fast food (whether it is purchased in a grocery store, vending machine, or restaurant) for the majority of their meals. Think about it. How many people do you know who might grab an Egg McMuffin® for breakfast, a Subway sandwich for lunch, and a Taco Bell burrito for dinner? Still sound a little improbable? How about grabbing a Pop-Tart for breakfast, bringing two or three slices of leftover pizza to school for lunch, getting some chips and a Coke from the vending machine for a snack, and cooking frozen, store-bought lasagna for dinner? That's already a day of fast food without even setting foot in a fast-food restaurant.

Educating Yourself

Eating three meals a day at McDonald's isn't representative of the average American diet, but fast food is far more prevalent in our lives than many people realize. Even fewer people fully comprehend the risks associated with so many of these foods. In response to criticisms, fast-food restaurants claim that nutrition information is widely available to the public. Many people, however, still don't have access to that information because it appears on companies' Web sites but is rarely posted in their restaurants. How often do you have access to the Internet while standing in line to purchase fast food? Furthermore, there are still plenty of Americans who do not have access to the Internet in their homes.

So let's educate ourselves. Let's take some of the menu items offered by just a few of the industry leaders: McDonald's, Burger King, Subway, Pizza Hut, and Taco Bell.

The United States Food and Drug Administration (FDA) requires food manufacturers meet specific guidelines if they wish to place claims like "low fat," "low cholesterol," "high fiber," "low sodium," "healthy," or others on their food labels. Look at the chart of FDA labeling requirements on page 61. Now examine the nutrition information for these fast foods. How many of them would meet the FDA's requirements for these health claims?

If you visit these restaurants' Web sites and look up their complete nutrition information, you will see that the foods included in this chart are neither the worst offenders (such as the McDonald's Deluxe Breakfast with 61 grams of fat or the Burger King DOUBLE WHOPPER® with cheese boasting 69 grams of fat) nor the least offensive options offered by these restaurants (such as a six-inch Subway Veggie Delite® sandwich with 3 grams of fat or a Taco Bell Fresco Style Soft Chicken Taco with 4 grams of fat). The items featured here are the middle-of-the-road foods—the types of foods that make up the bulk of these restaurants' menus. What do you notice? Of these twenty foods, only one—the Subway Sweet Onion Chicken Teriyaki Sandwich—would meet the FDA's requirements for a low-fat label. But look at what comes with that low-fat sandwich: 1,090 milligrams of sodium! The National Aca-demy of Sciences' Institute of Medicine recommends people consume less than 1,500 milligrams of sodium per day and never exceed 2,300 milligrams per day. With just one 6-inch low-fat sandwich, you've already consumed close to your daily allowance of sodium. In fact, out of these twenty items, eight will give you almost your entire day's worth of sodium, and two (the Burger King Fire-Grilled Shrimp Salad with dressing and the Subway Classic Club Salad with dressing) exceed your daily allowance.

These foods don't just come with extra salt. They also come with extra sugar. In fact, only two of these menu items (the McDonald's

Toxic Taco?
Horrific Hamburger?
What Is in That Food?

Food	Serving size (g.)	Calories	Total Fat (g.)	Sat. Fat (g.)	Chol. (mg)	Sodium (mg)	Carb. (g)	Fiber (g)	Sugar (g)	Protein (g)
McDonald's										
Big Mac ®	219	600	33	11	85	1050	50	4	8	25
Chicken McNuggets® (6 piece)	96	250	15	3	35	670	15	0	0	15
Grilled Chicken Bacon Ranch Salad (w/2 oz. Ranch dressing)	288	260	25	7	105	1460	18	3	7	32
Med. Fries	114	350	17	3	0	220	44	4	0	5
Burger King										
Original WHOPPER ®	291	700	42	13	85	1020	52	4	8	31
Original Chicken Sandwich	204	560	28	6	60	1270	52	3	5	25
Fire-Grilled Shrimp Garden Salad (w/2 oz. Sweet Onion Vinaigrette)	406	300	18	4	120	1860	21	3	13	21
Med. Onion Rings	91	320	16	4	0	460	40	3	5	4
Subway										
6" Sweet Onion Chicken Teriyaki Sandwich	271	370	5	1.5	50	1090	59	5	9	26
6" Meatball Marinara	288	500	22	11	45	1180	52	5	9	23
Classic Club Salad (w/1 packet Kraft Fat Free Italian dressing)	487	425	21	10	210	2540	20	4	9	38
Brown and Wild Rice w/ Chicken Soup	240	190	11	4.5	20	990	17	2	3	6
Pizza Hut										
1 Cheese Breadstick	67	200	10	3.5	15	340	21	1	4	7
12" Supreme Medium Pan Pizza (1 slice)	127	320	16	6	25	650		2	30	13
14" Sausage Lover's Stuffed Crust Pizza (1 Slice)	162	430	19	9	50	1130	43	3	9	19
12" Ham, Red Onion, and Mushroom Fit 'N Delicious (1 Slice)	101	160	4.5	2	15	470	22	2	6	8
Taco Bell										
Fresco Style Soft Beef Taco	113	190	8	3	20	630	22	3	3	9
Bean Burrito	198	370	10	3.5	10	1200	55	8	4	14
Chicken Chalupa Baja	153	400	24	6	40	690	30	2	4	17
Nachos Supreme	195	450	26	9	35	800	42	7	4	13

french fries and chicken nuggets) don't have added sugar. Even the salads have sugar! These sugar measurements don't even count the simple carbohydrates (which will be quickly converted to sugar in your body) contained in those squishy sesame seed buns or white-flour tortillas. Add a 16-ounce Coke (that's a small at McDonald's) and you add 40 grams of sugar.

And what about cholesterol? In chapter 2, you learned that your daily intake of cholesterol should not exceed 300 milligrams. Have one of the salads featured here, and you're already well on your way to that limit. Today, many fast-food restaurants advertise their salads as healthier alternatives to meaty burgers and sandwiches. This makes sense to consumers. Standing in line at a fast-food restaurant with no nutrition information in sight, wouldn't you assume the chicken or shrimp salads would be healthier than just about any burger or fries? You would be wrong. In this menu sample, the salads are the worst cholesterol offenders—and the offense can't all be attributed to loading up on fatty salad dressings. Even if you remove the dressing from the McDonald's, Burger King, and Subway salads shown in the chart, you still get 85, 120, and 210 milligrams of cholesterol, respectively. Go online and look at the other salads these restaurants offer. You'll probably be surprised to see that the ones featured here aren't even the worst examples.

Then, of course, there is the fat content of all of these foods. Some of them contain half or more of your daily intake of saturated fat, and nine of them contain over a third of the average person's daily intake of fat in general. What about the pizza, taco, or burrito? When it comes to fat, those aren't as bad as some . . . if you have just one. How many slices of pizza do you typically eat in a sitting? Might you order more than one taco or burrito? If you eat a couple of slices of pizza or multiple tacos and burritos, not only does your fat intake shoot up, your sodium levels go sky high. Furthermore, most of the items featured in this list are just main dishes. What happens if you begin adding side dishes or desserts to your burger? Add large fries, two packets of ketchup, and a large vanilla milk shake to a McDonald's sandwich, and you've added 1,290 Calories, 46 grams of fat (18.5 of them saturated), 90 milligrams of cholesterol, 1,100 milligrams of sodium, and 104 grams of sugar!

As we said in chapter 2, some fat is necessary in your diet, so a food that has a large amount of fat but little or no saturated fat (like McDonald's french fries) might not be so bad . . . except for one little catch: trans fats. When it comes to your health, trans fat is perhaps the worst type of fat there is (even worse than saturated fats), and it is plentiful in fast foods. Most trans fats (also known as hydrogenated or partially hydrogenated fats) do not occur in nature; they are human-made through a process called hydrogenation. In this process, hydrogen atoms are added to unsaturated fat molecules. The result is unsaturated fats that stay solid at room temperature. Basically, they have been transformed to saturated fats.

Make Connections: Like eating plastic?

To make liquid unsaturated fats into solids, hydrogen atoms are added to the molecules. You could compare this to the production of plastic. Plastic starts out as liquid, petroleum-based oils. The molecular structure of this liquid oil is changed to make it into the solid we call plastic. In fact, some doctors actually compare the stiff, indigestible trans fats to plastic! Many people's love affair with trans fat has now soured. Some countries are considering banning them from food products all together. The United States, however, has not been nearly so **proactive**. Under pressure from different interest groups and consumers, some companies are already listing the amounts of trans fats in their foods, and other companies like Kraft have promised to reduce or eliminate the amount of trans fats in their products. Regulation, however, is not yet mandatory.

Hydrogenated fats are extremely important to the fast-food industry because they increase the shelf-life of food and are very cheap. Many natural fats spoil quickly if they are not refrigerated. Some hydrogenated fats can stay unrefrigerated for months or even years without spoiling! They also make things taste good. They appear in everything from fast food, to breakfast cereal, to pretzels, to candy, and until recently, companies promoted hydrogenated fats as a healthy alternative to saturated fats. But our bodies have a hard time metabolizing trans fats. Because they are manmade, they are foreign to our bodies' digestive systems. Our bodies can't recognize what trans fats are or figure out what to do with them. Instead of being broken down into energy and removed from the body, hydrogenated fats get packed away. They clog up the system! They can even build up along the walls of your blood vessels and on the surface of your brain, increasing your risk for heart attack and stroke. They also increase your LDL cholesterol while lowering your HDL cholesterol.

Right now, North American food manufacturers are not required to list trans fats on food labels, but that doesn't mean they are not there. Look on ingredients labels for the words "hydrogenated" or "partially hydrogenated." Anything with these oils in the ingredients list contains trans fats and should be avoided. Currently, McDonald's and Burger King cook all of their fried foods in partially hydrogenated vegetable oils, but that's not the only place trans fats appear. Besides the fries, chicken nuggets, hash browns, and any other item dipped into the deep fryer, trans fats make an appearance in every single McDonald's sandwich (partially hydrogenated oils are used in all of McDonald's buns); all the breakfast items except the bagel, hotcakes, and sausage; and six of the ten salads. Add margarine to the bagel and hotcakes or buttered croutons to the other salads, and they have trans fats as well. Trans fats show up in the vast majority of Burger King's menu items as well, but at least Burger King **discloses** the amount of trans fat in their nutrition information. Subway scores higher when it comes to trans fats, but they still use partially hydrogenated oils in four of their breads, the chicken breast patty, the meatballs, some salad toppings, and all their cookies. Pizza Hut and Taco Bell neither list trans fats on their nutrition guides nor provide detailed ingredient information for their foods, so it is impossible to know how extensive the use of trans fats is in their menus.

After a thorough examination of these five restaurants' entire menus, you would find that only four food items could meet the FDA's requirements for a "healthy" label. They are McDonald's side salad with no dressing and Newman's Own® Salsa (you could put this on your side salad for a little extra flavor), Burger King's side salad with no dressing, and Subway's Garden Fresh salad with no dressing. Pizza Hut and Taco Bell have nothing "healthy" to offer.

Of course, you don't have to eat 100 percent healthy food 100 percent of the time. We all indulge now and again, and it can be important to do so. You should enjoy your food, and having a hamburger or a milk shake once in a while can be very satisfying. There are two problems, however. The first is

In the last ten years, a new type of fast food has exploded on the market: so-called "energy" foods like protein bars and electrolyte-replenishing drinks. These foods are often marketed as the "power within athletes," but a study by Consumlab.com (an independent research group that provides information to consumers and health professionals) found that 60 percent of the "nutrition" bars they studied didn't live up to the claims made on their labels. Energy drinks may not be much better. Take a look, for example, at Gatorade, that so-called energy drink for replenishing electrolytes after exercise. If you look at Gatorade's ingredient label you will see that it contains sodium and potassium, two of the essential electrolytes that keep your muscles working. Sodium might be an electrolyte, but too much of it is dangerous for your health. The average American diet already contains at least twice the recommended daily intake of sodium; you don't need to be drinking it in a "sports drink." But what else will you find? The number-one ingredient in Gatorade (after water) is sugar. Look a little further down the list: hydrogenated soybean and cottonseed oils! Your "healthy" energy drink contains trans fats!

Text-Dependent Questions:

1. Why is it healthier to eat foods in their original forms than after they have been processed?
2. Why are vitamins and minerals often added to breads and cereal?
3. Is fast food only limited to fast-food restaurants?
4. Explain why fast-food salads are often as unhealthy for you as a burger.
5. Why don't our bodies recognize trans fats?

that we've become so accustomed to fast foods, both in restaurants and grocery stores, and have so little knowledge about what is in them that we end up indulging all the time without even realizing we are doing so. The second problem, and this is one of the biggest, is portion size. In the past fifteen years, portion sizes for fast foods have increased so dramatically that many people no longer realize what an acceptable portion of food even is. Next, we'll take a closer look at this **phenomenon** and explore its role in the obesity crisis.

Words to Understand

stereotype: A preconceived and oversimplified impression of the characteristics that define a person, group, or situation.

foraging: Wandering in search of food.

Western: Of Western Europe and North America.

coalesced: Came together to form a whole.

service-based economy: A market system that relies on the provision of services rather than the manufacture of goods.

sedentary: Characterized by much time sitting and little time moving.

profit margins: Differences between the cost of buying or producing something and the price at which it is sold.

agricultural subsidies: Money given by the government to support certain farms or crops.

mantras: Frequently repeated words, phrases, or slogans.

Chapter 5

Big Mac Nation
Going Supersized

- An American Stereotype
- The Ever-Increasing Portion
- Profit and Portions
- Skewed Hunger Mechanisms

An American Stereotype

If you have ever traveled outside of the United States, you may have noticed an interesting phenomenon. Perhaps you went into a coffee shop or a restaurant and ordered a beverage. Maybe you ordered a small size because that is what you normally order at home in the United States. When you got your small drink, you may have blinked twice. It was really, really small! Or perhaps you ordered a large, because that is what you normally order at home. If so, then you definitely blinked twice, and perhaps you said, "Excuse me. I ordered a large, not a small." If so, your Americanness was suddenly on display for everyone to see.

Most Americans never travel outside of America, so we don't necessarily realize that other people around the world don't eat or live as we do. In fact, America is quite famous around the world for its "bigness." "In America," people say, "everything is big—big country, big houses, big cars, big money, big food, big drinks, and big people." On the one hand, this is a **stereotype**, and stereotypes are never all true. On the other hand, stereotypes sometimes arise from actual circumstances, and in the case of American fast food the stereotypes are largely right.

The Ever-Increasing Portion

Today the portion sizes you encounter in fast-food restaurants are many times the size they were just twenty or even ten years ago. In some cases, they have grown grossly out of proportion with the human body. A study published by the *Journal of the American Medical Association* found that between the years 1971 and 1999, portion

sizes for certain foods increased dramatically. Of the foods studied—hamburgers, Mexican food, soft drinks, snacks, and pizza—all but pizza increased. Hamburgers became, on average, more than a fifth larger. A plate of Mexican food was more than one-quarter larger. Soft drinks had expanded by more than half their previous size, and salty snacks like potato chips, pretzels, and crackers had grown by 60 percent. The most striking increases occurred in, you guessed it, fast-food restaurants. Most disturbingly, however, the portion increases did not stop there. The study found that these portion increases occurred in the American home as well. Whether eating out or eating in, Americans are eating more than ever before, and you can bet that those extra Calories are a factor in the rising obesity crisis.

Increasing portion sizes would be disturbing just on their own, but combined with another factor—decreasing activity—they are especially alarming. We Americans are not only eating more than ever before, we're also less active than we've ever been. The human body did not evolve to sit in a car, behind a desk, in front of a computer, or before a television. Yet for many of us, these are exactly the activities that take up most of our time. For about 99 percent of human history (and still for most humans in the world today), people never had to consciously think about exercising because their whole lives involved exercise. **Foraging** and hunting took huge amounts of energy. Farming is also exhausting, back-breaking, Calorie-burning work. Even with the rise of the industrial age, when many people in the **Western** world left farming to make money in mines, factories, and industry-driven trades, most of the work was still just as physical and exhausting.

It's really only within the last fifty to sixty years that American lifestyles changed so dramatically. In this time, numerous factors have **coalesced** to produce our inactive lifestyle. A flight to the suburbs has made us reliant on cars to get to work, school, grocery stores, friends' houses, and other destinations, whereas our previous urban living allowed for walking and bicycling. A switch to a **service-based economy** has put more of us in offices and **sedentary** jobs. With much of our time spent at work, the only time left

for exercise is leisure time. But technologies like televisions and computers have made much of our leisure time sedentary as well. Just because much of our work is no longer physical, however, doesn't mean it's not exhausting, and after a long day at school or work, most of us find it easier to plop down in front of the television than go exercise.

The movement toward a sedentary lifestyle is definitely contributing to the rise in obesity. Remember our discussion of Calories in chapter 2? There we said that the average active woman needs about 2,200 Calories each day, while the average active man needs 2,800 Calories each day. In a perfect world, we would all be active, but our world is not perfect. Most Americans live inactive lives. If you are an inactive woman, you will probably only need 1,500 to 1,800 Calories each day, while an inactive man will likely only need 2,000 to 2,200. That's a big difference from active people, and growing portion sizes aren't helping us keep our caloric intake in line with our activity levels. For people who eat fast food on a regular basis, increasing exercise alone may not be able to counteract all the extra Calories in those big portions. An increase in activity has to be combined with a decrease in caloric intake.

Profit and Portions

If you had kept track of packaged foods sold in grocery stores over the last few years, you would have noticed an interesting trend. While portion sizes at home and in fast-food restaurants have been increasing, the amount of food in some grocery store products has been decreasing. These decreases (where they have occurred) have been small. You may not even be able to detect them simply by looking at the food. But if you start reading labels, you will see that half an ounce has disappeared from that can, 20 grams has been deducted from that box, a few millimeters have been shaved from that candy bar.

Many of the foods sold in grocery stores have very low **profit margins**. After production, processing, and shipping, a company may spend dollars to produce a certain food and then be able to sell it for only a few cents more. Companies that only make a few cents' profit for every dollar they spend have realized they can increase their profits by removing just a little bit of food from the package. They don't, however, charge you less for this slightly smaller amount of food, so suddenly they are making more money by selling you less product. By putting a little less food in every package, they make just a couple more cents (or maybe only fractions of a cent).

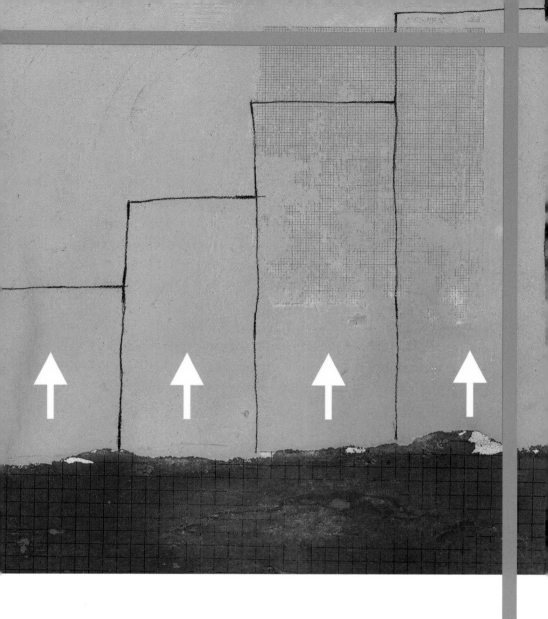

But add those fractions and cents up over thousands or even millions of sales, and suddenly you see a substantial increase in profits. So if size reduction has maximized profits for some food manufacturers, why have fast-food restaurants gone in the opposite direction? Why are their portion sizes increasing?

Companies that sell expensive foods can make more money by giving their customers less. Fast-food restaurants are just the opposite. Unlike many foods sold in grocery stores or upper-scale sit-down restaurants, the profit margins for fast foods can be huge. **Agricultural subsidies**, tax breaks, mass production, low labor costs, and other cost-saving systems make their food so plentiful and so cheap that they can't gain anything by withholding it from you. Some of these foods only cost restaurants pennies, but they sell them to you for dollars. Think about this example. Imagine that taking away half the fries in your large order would save the restaurant ten cents. Ten cents from every customer would certainly add up over time. After serving millions of customers, those dimes would become huge profits. But now think about this scenario. If the restaurant gives you twice as many fries, it will only cost ten cents more. But, and this is a big but, if they can get you to pay thirty cents more for those extra fries, they have just made twenty cents in profit—twice as much as they would have gotten from decreasing portion sizes! For fast-food restaurants, bigger portion sizes mean bigger profits.

When McDonald's first began, it didn't even have medium and large options. Fries were fries, and they came in what today would look like a very small package. When fast-food restaurants realized that they could increase their profits dramatically by giving you more food and just charging you a little more for it, larger sizes were born. Slogans like "Get more for your money!" and "Bigger is better!" became fast-food **mantras**. Suddenly everyone was on board. "Value meals" came next. Wendy's introduced Biggie® drinks and Biggie® fries. Then Biggie® wasn't big enough, and they introduced Great Biggie®. McDonald's introduced Supersize®. Burger King had King drinks and King fries. In some restaurants, what was once a regular-size fries or drink is now the "kiddie size," and what used to be a large is now a small!

In Fast Food Nation, Eric Schlosser reports that a medium Coke at McDonald's contains 9 cents' worth of syrup (the rest is simply carbonated water, which costs close to nothing). A large Coke contains 12 cents' worth of syrup. How much do you normally pay for a medium or large Coke at McDonald's?

Skewed Hunger Mechanisms

In chapter 2, we discussed your body's natural mechanisms for telling you whether you were hungry or full. Recently, researchers at Penn State University's College of Health and Human Development wanted to see if people's hunger mechanisms would stand up to increased portion sizes. In their study, they gave volunteers large portions of macaroni and cheese and told them to eat until they were full. The results astounded the researchers. When the volunteers were given smaller portions, they stopped eating sooner, even if they didn't clean their plates. When given a larger portion, the volunteers ate an average of 30 percent more (again even if they didn't clean their plates) and did not report feeling fuller. The volunteers did not realize they had eaten more at the large-portion sittings, and most didn't even notice the portion size had increased.

The fast-food industry claims they have no responsibility in America's obesity crisis and that individuals must take personal responsibility for what they eat. At the same time, however, we can see that taking that personal responsibility can be difficult if we don't know what is in the food and are faced with constantly increasing portion sizes. There's another problem, however, when the fast-food industry claims its foods and practices aren't responsible for America's obesity crisis and that individuals have to take their health into their own hands. Fast-food restaurants are businesses, and a business's goal is to make money—as much money as possible. Fast-food restaurants, therefore, can't encourage you not to eat their food! If they did, and if you listened, they couldn't make any money! Today the fast-food giants are huge corporations that take in billions of dollars every year. These corporations are all in competition with each other for your business. They don't want you to be "responsible" fast-food consumers who only eat their unhealthy food on rare occasions. They want you to eat lots of their food and eat it often.

Research Project

Think of the most popular occupations today. Do any of these require extensive physical activity? Now go to the library and find out which occupations were the most common in the 1950s. Are these more physically demanding? Write down how the occupations differed between these two time periods, and connect how obesity may have increased from the 1950s to today.

To encourage you to do this, they employ a very powerful tool: advertising. In fact, the fast-food industry spends billions of dollars every year on advertising, and they're not advertising side salads with no dressing. As we will see in the next chapter, the fast-food industry may claim that you have sole responsibility for what you eat, but they employ some powerful techniques in an effort to help you exercise that responsibility.

Words to Understand

ingratiated: Gained favor through deliberate effort.
disposable income: The amount of money available after expenses are paid.
inaccessible: Cannot be reached.
stipulate: Demand, specify, or require.
quotas: Quantities that must be produced.
accomplices: Partners.

Chapter 6

Out of the Television . . .

- And into Your Home
- And into Your Schools

And into Your Home

In chapter 1, we talked about Richard and Maurice (the founders of McDonald's) and Ray Kroc (the man who transformed McDonald's into the powerful corporation it is today). Well, the story didn't stop there. After a few years, Ray Kroc got sick of Richard and Maurice. Kroc was out building an empire, but it wasn't his empire. It was the McDonalds' empire, and Richard and Maurice were sitting at home holding veto power over Kroc's decisions. In 1961, Kroc and the McDonalds made a deal. He bought their share of the business for 2.7 million dollars, and they retained ownership of their original restaurant. After a number of years, Kroc opened a McDonald's across the street from that restaurant and ran Richard and Maurice out of business.

Today, there are thousands upon thousands of fast-food restaurants across the United States. In fact, you can drive through sections of many towns and find a fast-food restaurant on every corner. This means stiff competition. The best tool the fast-food industry has to get your business is advertising. When it comes to advertising, fast-food restaurants hold no punches. They spend billions of dollars every year trying to convince you that their food is irresistible.

Over the years, advertising has changed in an important way. It used to be almost solely directed at adults. The reason was quite logical. Adults have the jobs, and adults have the money, so messages about where to spend that money should be aimed at those adults. But fast-food companies realized something early on. Children usually have more influence with their parents than companies have. If a fast-food company could get children to want a product, those children would go to their parents, beg and plead, and often be successful in gaining what they wanted. When an advertisement aimed at

an adult was successful, it might bring in one customer. When an advertisement aimed at a child was successful, it often brought in three or more customers (the child and the child's parents and siblings). Marketing to children, of course, is in no way limited to the fast-food industry. Today, all kinds of manufacturers, from those who make toys to those who make cars, realize that the best way to get into Mom and Dad's pocket is through their child. Kids mean big money.

Companies that advertised to children learned another important lesson: a child converted will be a customer for life. Companies believed that if they could get a child to become loyal to their brand and products early on, that

child would remain loyal for the rest of his life. A child who started eating McDonald's before he tasted Burger King, the theory went, would continue eating McDonald's. A child who started drinking Coke before she tasted Pepsi would always prefer Coke. A person who had pleasant memories of slurping milk shakes as a child would slurp milk shakes as an adult. The companies were right. Brand loyalty, a person's commitment to a specific brand, often has less to do with the actual quality of the product than with how early and successfully the brand can be **ingratiated** into the person's consciousness.

Like so many other fast-food trends, McDonald's was the first—and for a long time it remained the leader—in advertising to children. Ronald McDonald, Hamburgler, and other characters appeared frequently during children's television programming. McDonaldlands and Playlands promised safe and wholesome fun for children, and Happy Meals complete with toys promised . . . well, happiness to kids.

McDonald's may have led the trend, but everyone else quickly caught on. The messages too became more varied. Soon advertisements aimed at parents portrayed bringing your kids to a fast-food restaurant as a sign of good parenting, a way to make up for spending so much time at work and away from the family, and a way to increase children's love and affection. Advertisements to children stressed the benefits for their parents—the food would be tasty, fast, and affordable—thereby arming the kids with ammunition. The advertisements basically coached kids on what to say to convince their parents that going out for fast food is a good idea.

These forms of advertising are by no means limited to the fast food sold in restaurants. They are used to sell the packaged foods in vending machines and grocery stores as well. According to Marion Nestle of New York University's Department of Nutrition and Food Studies, about half of all

> "The challenge of the campaign is to make customers believe that McDonald's is their 'Trusted Friend.'"
>
> –Ray Bergold, McDonald's marketing executive

advertisements directed toward children are for food. She estimates that the food and drink industries spend $13 billion each year advertising to kids.

Today, all kinds of people are employed in the business of marketing to children, and they use numerous tools to figure out how. Psychiatrists give analysis of children's dreams. Researchers explore the effects of bright colors on the child brain. Artists and designers develop eye-catching logos and child-friendly characters. Young children are largely powerless against this onslaught. Studies have shown that young children can't distinguish between regular television entertainment and commercials. They don't know that they are being seduced by advertising and that their minds, emotions, and desires are being carefully manipulated by people with huge amounts of money, research, and expertise. They also don't yet have the skills to determine if advertising claims are trustworthy or not. If you tell a young child that a candy bar will make her strong, for example, she will believe you. Children are defenseless against advertising, and fast-food corporations know it. According to James McNeal, author of *Kids as Customers* and *The Kids' Market: Myths and Realities*, companies begin influencing children when they are as young as two years old. By the time they are three, many children can recognize brand logos. Furthermore, exhausted parents often feel defenseless against children's constant nagging. Fast-food corporations know this too and put lots of research money into finding the best way to exploit what they call the "nag factor."

Young children, however, aren't the only ones being targeted by advertising. In the last twenty years, teens have emerged as a huge market force. Besides money received as allowances or gifts, many teens work. Teens today have more **disposable income** than they have ever had before. Each year, teens spend more than $150 billion from their own pockets. That's a huge amount of money, and fast-food companies want to get their share. To make sure they are getting as much of young people's money as possible, food and drink corporations have embarked on a huge and disturbing trend.

And into Your Schools

Many American schools have faced serious financial difficulties in recent decades. Cuts in government spending, opposition to tax increases, and increasing enrollments have left some schools gasping for funds. When food and soft drink manufacturers began offering thousands of dollars for the privilege of getting their products and advertisements into the schools, many districts rushed to sign up. Advertising on television and in print was good, but young people still had the power to turn off the TV or put the magazine down. Furthermore, if they're not on summer vacation, young people are spending most of each day at school where they can't watch television or read magazines. If food

Research Project

Over the course of one day, write down all of the advertisements for food that you see. They could be commercials, posters, vending machines, or billboards. At the end of the day, count up all of the advertisements that you wrote down. Create a chart and mark down which age group each of the advertisements was targeting. Were some focusing on children under the age of twelve? Maybe they were trying to get teenagers to spend some extra money at their restaurant, or hoping they could get adults to stop by and try a new flavor of coffee. Did the advertisements convince you to stop by a fast-food restaurant?

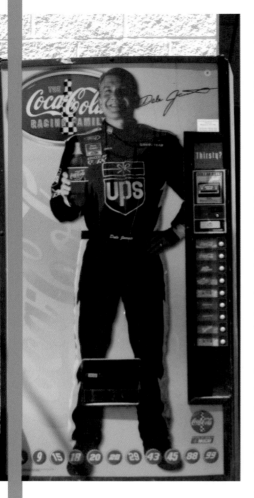

and beverage companies could get into the schools, they could not only reach children and teens during this otherwise **inaccessible** part of the day, they could have them as a captive audience. After all, you can't just walk out of a school because you don't want to see an advertisement.

Today, food and beverage companies not only have their vending machines in the hallways, advertisements on the walls, billboards on school buses, and logos plastered at sports events; they have also taken over many school lunch programs. America's government-sponsored school lunch program was never completely healthy to begin with, but today it has definitely taken a turn for the worse. For many schools, gone are the days of sloppy joes, mashed potatoes, apples, and cartons of milk. Today, many children and teens go to the school cafeteria to grab pizza, cheeseburgers, chips, Coke, Pepsi, and fries. Depending on their contracts, schools may even get a percentage of the fast-food or beverage sales. Worse yet, some schools have contracts that **stipulate** minimum sales **quotas**; if those quotas aren't met, the school can lose some of the promised revenues. This has led to some schools allowing soft drinks and snacks to be purchased in the hallways and consumed in the classrooms. The need for money to support their programs has turned some schools into **accomplices** of the food and beverage industries. Many schools now work with these industries to encourage fast-food consumption and maximize sales.

The presence of fast foods in schools **undermines** parents' ability to

Text-Dependent Questions:

1. Why did fast-food restaurants start targeting children in their advertisements?
2. Why do companies spend billions of dollars on advertising?
3. Why have teens recently been targeted by advertising?
4. Why did schools agree to put up posters and signs advertising fast food and soft drinks?

make healthy food choices for their children. More than that, it gives fast-food and beverage companies easy access to young people whose eating habits and lifestyles are still developing. Studies show that the habits we form when we are young usually stay with us for life and are the most difficult to break. A person who starts smoking at a young age will fight a difficult battle if she wants to quit and may very well end up smoking for life. Similarly, a person who starts eating fast food and drinking sugary soft drinks on a regular basis early on will carry those eating habits into adulthood and may end up fighting a lifelong battle against obesity.

Words to Understand

virulence: Extreme aggressiveness; ability to spread quickly and overpower.

pathogens: Things that cause disease.

benevolent: Charitable; actively friendly.

type 2 diabetes: A disease caused by the lack of or inefficient use of insulin, usually occurring in adulthood, but being increasingly seen in teenagers and younger children.

economics: The financial considerations associated with a particular activity, commodity, etc.

Chapter 7

Fighting the Fast Food Habit: Can America Downsize?

- The Obesity Lifestyle
- Who Has Time to Bake Whole-Wheat Muffins?
- What Can You Do?

The Obesity Lifestyle

Shortly after the film *Supersize Me* premiered, McDonald's did away with its famous "supersize" option. They claimed their decision had nothing to do with the film and was motivated by consumer trends. McDonald's isn't the only one feeling a consumer backlash against the unhealthiness of their foods and the **virulence** of their advertising practices. Some school districts have begun kicking the food and beverage industries out of their schools. Kraft, one of America's largest food manufacturers, recently promised to start cutting portion sizes of single-serving snacks. McDonald's and Kraft are also studying the issue of trans fats in their foods and may make moves to reduce the heart-clogging agents. Recently, the cookie manufacturer Voortman became the first North American food manufacturer to completely eliminate trans fats from their products. All of these are good moves, but are they enough to combat America's growing obesity crisis?

Unfortunately, the answer is no. Certainly, moves by industry leaders to remove **pathogens** from their products and cut ridiculously large portion sizes are good steps and should be applauded. But America today is so deeply entrenched in its fast-food habit that even these positive changes are not going to shrink growing waistlines or give us all healthier, more active lifestyles. Furthermore, companies are not simply making **benevolent** changes for the benefits of our bottoms. They make changes for the benefit of their bottom line. As long as a company feels it can keep making more money by producing unhealthy foods than it can make producing healthy foods, it will keep to the tried and true unhealthy track. Although some companies are seeing the profit potential in going healthy, in the end companies will always be profit motivated, so you cannot simply trust them to make good decisions for your health. That's something only you can do.

America is suffering from an obesity crisis, but in the end, it doesn't matter whether you personally struggle with your weight or not. We all contribute to the epidemic when we frequent fast-food restaurants that serve unhealthy fare, purchase products laden with trans fats, and plop down in front of the television instead of going outside. Plenty of people look slim on the outside but are still living the obesity lifestyle and paying for it with their health. Obesity is easy to see, but high cholesterol, heart disease, **type 2 diabetes**, and other lifestyle-related illnesses can be invisible and deadly. So how can you start? How can you shake the fast-food habit?

Who Has Time to Bake Whole-Wheat Muffins?

So many of our unhealthy eating habits are based on lack of time, necessity, and sometimes skewed priorities. In many American families, both parents have to work. Many other American families are single-parent households. With situations like these, few families have the time to make healthy food from scratch. At the same time, we are bombarded by media messages telling us we need to have all kinds of "great" things. If we want these "great" things, however, we must spend even more time working to make the money for all these things, which leads to even less time for important things like eating healthfully. At the same time, one of the things the media messages tell us we need to have is fast foods and convenience foods. Since we are pressed for time anyway, we latch on to these convenient products—products that are tasty, filling, and leave us always hungry for more, but which are really void of nutrition and packed with empty calories.

It's not impossible to have fast foods in our diet and still be healthy. After all, fast food comes in a wide variety—from saturated fat-laden burgers to organic dried fruit snacks. But having fast food as a part of a healthy lifestyle means giving up almost all restaurant fast food and taking the time to seek

Research Project

Think of some of the most popular brand name products that people buy, such as Kraft and Pepsi. Write down as many as you can think of. Then go online and find if they use trans fats in their products. Are any of the companies trying to phase out trans fats? Have any been successful? Create a chart, marking which companies still use trans fats, which are attempting to remove them from their products, and which no longer have them in the list of ingredients.

out products that have no trans fats, are low in simple carbohydrates and saturated fats, and are high in fiber and nutrients. When such foods can't be found, we need to take the time to make such foods ourselves. Then we also need to find the time to increase our activity levels. But all this makes it sound like the fast-food industry is right—that the key to solving the obesity crisis is all about personal responsibility.

Not quite. Yes, you have to take personal responsibility for the foods you put in your mouth every day and the amount of time you spend being physically active. But as we've said throughout this book, other powerful forces are at work as well, and someone needs to rein in those forces. How can you as an individual compete against billions of dollars of advertising, federal regulations that protect the fast-food and drink industries, an onslaught of unhealthy products in your school, and **economics** that make the most unhealthy foods the most affordable? Clearly, you can't take on all these issues alone. Something bigger has to change—but you can help.

What Can You Do?

Now you are armed with a little bit of knowledge. Get even more informed. Go to fast-food company websites and learn what's really in their products. Write to companies and tell them you refuse to buy their products until they offer you healthy options—more options than simply a side salad with no dressing. Switch your business to companies that do offer healthy options, and let them and other companies know why you are making this decision. Write to your senators and representatives and let them know you support legislation that would place restrictions on advertising directed at children and would require food companies to reveal the trans fats in their products. If you are old enough to vote, or when you become old enough to vote, get informed about candidates' positions on important issues like Americans' health, and vote for the candidates who support your ideas. If fast foods are in your school, start asking why. Bring a bagged lunch and let your school know why you are doing so. When advertisements for fast foods come on television, press the mute button and spend the next minute doing a few jumping jacks or explaining to your younger siblings why that beautiful, juicy item of food splashed across the television screen may not be healthy. Help educate your parents. Study after study shows that the biggest influences on children and their behaviors are their parents.

You can't take on the huge issue of America's obesity crisis alone, but by making some changes in your own life, adopting healthier exercise and eating habits, and refusing to give your money to the manufacturers of unhealthy foods, you can begin to fight the fast-food habit.

Series Glossary of Key Terms

Aerobic exercise: Activities that use large muscle groups (back, chest, and legs) to increase heart rate and breathing for an extended period of time, such as bicycling, brisk walking, running, and swimming. Federal guidelines recommend that adults get 150 to 300 minutes of aerobic activity a week.

Body mass index (BMI): A measure of body weight relative to height that uses a mathematical formula to get a score to determine if a person is underweight, at a normal weight, overweight, or obese. For adults, a BMI of 18.5 to 24.9 is considered healthy; a person with a BMI of 25 to 29.9 is considered overweight, and a person with a BMI of 30 or more is considered obese. BMI charts for children compare their height and weight to other children of their same sex and age.

Calorie: A unit of energy in food.

Carbohydrate: A type of food that is a major source of energy for your body. Your digestive system changes carbohydrates into blood glucose (sugar). Your body uses this sugar to make energy for cells, tissues, and organs, and stores any extra sugar in your liver and muscles for when it is needed. If there is more sugar than the body can use, it is stored as body fat.

Cholesterol: A fat-like substance that is made by your body and found naturally in animal foods such as dairy products, eggs, meat, poultry, and seafood. Foods high in cholesterol include dairy fats, egg yolks, and organ meats such as liver. Cholesterol is needed to carry out functions such as hormone and vitamin production, but too much can build up inside arteries, increasing the risk of heart disease.

Diabetes: A person with this disease has blood glucose—sugar—levels that are above normal levels. Insulin is a hormone that helps the glucose get into your cells to give them energy. Diabetes occurs when the body does not make enough insulin or does not use the insulin it makes. Over time, having too much sugar in your blood may cause serious problems. It may damage your eyes, kidneys, and nerves, and may cause heart disease and stroke. Regular physical activity, weight control, and healthy eating helps to control or prevent diabetes.

Diet: What a person eats and drinks. It may also be a type of eating plan.

Fat: A major source of energy in the diet that also helps the body absorb fat-soluble vitamins, such as vitamins A, D, E, and K.

High blood pressure: Blood pressure refers to the way blood presses against the blood vessels as it flows through them. With high blood pressure, the heart works harder, and the chances of a stroke, heart attack, and kidney problems are greater.

Metabolism: The process that occurs in the body to turn the food you eat into energy your body can use.

Nutrition: The process of the body using food to sustain life.

Obesity: Excess body fat that is more than 20 percent of what is considered to be healthy.

Overweight: Excess body fat that is more than 10 to 20 percent of what is considered to be healthy.

Portion size: The amount of a food served or eaten in one occasion. A portion is not a standard amount (it's different from a "serving size"). The amount of food it includes may vary by person and occasion.

Protein: One of the nutrients in food that provides calories to the body. Protein is an essential nutrient that helps build many parts of the body, including blood, bone, muscle, and skin. It is found in foods like beans, dairy products, eggs, fish, meat, nuts, poultry, and tofu.

Saturated fat: This type of fat is solid at room temperature. It is found in foods like full-fat dairy products, coconut oil, lard, and ready-to-eat meats. Eating a diet high in saturated fat can raise blood cholesterol and increase the risk of heart disease.

Serving size: A standard amount of a food, such as a cup or an ounce.

Stroke: When blood flow to your brain stops, causing brain cells to begin to die.

Trans fats: A type of fat produced when liquid fats (oils) are turned into solid fats through a chemical process called hydrogenation. Eating a large amount of trans fats raises blood cholesterol and increases the risk of heart disease.

Unsaturated fat: These healthier fats are liquid at room temperature. Vegetable oils are a major source of unsaturated fat. Other foods, such as avocados, fatty fish like salmon and tuna, most nuts, and olives are good sources of unsaturated fat.

Whole grains: Grains and grain products made from the entire grain seed; usually a good source of dietary fiber.

Further Reading

Kittler, Pamela Goyan. *Food and Culture*. Stamford, CT: Cengage, 2011.

Polan, Michael. *Food Rules: An Eater's Manual*. New York: Penguin, 2009.

Smith, Andrew F. *Encyclopedia of Junk Food and Fast Food*. Westport, CT: Greenwood, 2006.

Spurlock, Morgan. *Don't Eat This Book: Fast Food and the Supersizing of America*. New York: Berkley, 2006.

———. *Supersized: Strange Tales from a Fast-Food Culture*. Milwaukie, OR: Dark Horse Comics, 2010.

Weber, Karl, editor. *Food, Inc: How Industrial Food Is Making Us Sicker, Fatter, and Poorer—and What You Can Do About It*. New York: Public Affairs, 2009.

Wilson, Charles and Eric Schlosser. *Chew on This: Everything You Don't Want to Know About Fast Food*. New York: HMH Books, 2013.

For More Information

Burger King's Nutrition Information
www.bk.com/en/us/menu-nutrition/index.html

Comparison of the USDA's Food Guide Pyramid with Harvard's Healthy
Eating Pyramid
www.hsph.harvard.edu/nutritionsource/pyramid

McDonald's Nutrition Information
www.mcdonalds.com/usa/eat/nutrition_info.html

National Center for Chronic Disease Prevention and Health Promotion's
Information on Obesity
www.cdc.gov/obesity/index.html

Pizza Hut's Nutrition Information
www.pizzahut.com/nutrition.html

Subway's Nutrition Information
www.subway.com/nutrition/nutritionlist.aspx

Taco Bell's Nutrition Information
www.tacobell.com/nutrition/information

Publisher's note:
The websites listed on these pages were active at the time of publication. The
publisher is not responsible for websites that have changed their addresses or
discontinued operation since the date of publication. The publisher will review
the websites and update the list upon each reprint.

Index

About the Author and the Consultant

Autumn Libal received her degree from Smith College in Northampton, MA. A former water-aerobics instructor, she now dedicates herself exclusively to writing for young people. Other Mason Crest series she has contributed to include PSYCHIATRIC DISORDERS: DRUGS & PSYCHOLOGY FOR THE MIND AND BODY, YOUTH WITH SPECIAL NEEDS, and THE SCIENCE OF HEALTH: YOUTH AND WELL-BEING. She has also written health-related articles for *New Moon: The Magazine for Girls and Their Dreams*.

Dr. Victor F. Garcia is the co-director of the Comprehensive Weight Management Center at Cincinnati Children's Hospital Medical Center. He is a board member of Discover Health of Greater Cincinnati, a fellow of the American College of Surgeons, and a two-time winner of the Martin Luther King Humanitarian Award.

Picture Credits